50 Italian Pizza Recipes for Home

By: Kelly Johnson

Table of Contents

- Margherita Pizza
- Pepperoni Pizza
- Quattro Stagioni Pizza
- Capricciosa Pizza
- Funghi Pizza
- Diavola Pizza
- Napoletana Pizza
- Prosciutto e Rucola Pizza
- Pizza Bianca with Ricotta and Spinach
- Pizza Marinara
- Pizza Siciliana
- Pizza Romana
- Pizza alla Puttanesca
- Veggie Supreme Pizza
- Pizza al Salame
- Pizza al Pesto
- Pizza Boscaiola
- Pizza Rustica
- Calzone with Ricotta and Ham
- Pizza al Tartufo
- Pizza Napoli with Anchovies
- Pizza con Gorgonzola e Pere
- Pizza with Mushrooms and Truffle Oil
- Pizza Margherita with Burrata
- Pizza alla Caprese
- Pizza with Sausage and Peppers
- Pizza alla Norma
- Pizza with Prosciutto di Parma and Figs
- Pizza with Grilled Vegetables
- Pizza ai Quattro Formaggi
- Pizza con Pomodorini e Basilico
- Pizza with Smoked Salmon and Cream Cheese
- Pizza with Eggplant and Mozzarella
- Pizza with Pancetta and Pears
- Pizza Capricciosa with Artichokes

- Pizza with Zucchini and Ricotta
- Pizza with Sautéed Spinach and Garlic
- Pizza with Fennel and Sausage
- Pizza alla Salsiccia e Friarielli
- Pizza con Radicchio e Gorgonzola
- Pizza with Fresh Basil and Mozzarella
- Pizza ai Frutti di Mare
- Pizza with Sweet Potatoes and Goat Cheese
- Pizza with Roasted Red Peppers and Olives
- Pizza with Chicken and Pesto
- Pizza Margherita with Arugula
- Pizza with Speck and Apples
- Pizza alla Diavola with Chili Peppers
- Pizza with Ricotta, Honey, and Pistachios
- Pizza with Roasted Garlic and Parmesan

Margherita Pizza

Ingredients:

- Pizza dough
- 1/2 cup tomato sauce
- 1 1/2 cups fresh mozzarella, sliced
- Fresh basil leaves
- Olive oil for drizzling
- Salt to taste

Instructions:

1. Preheat the oven to 475°F (245°C).
2. Roll out the pizza dough on a floured surface.
3. Spread a thin layer of tomato sauce on the dough, leaving a small border for the crust.
4. Top with fresh mozzarella slices.
5. Bake for 10-12 minutes, or until the crust is golden and the cheese is bubbly.
6. Once out of the oven, scatter fresh basil leaves over the top and drizzle with olive oil. Serve immediately.

Pepperoni Pizza

Ingredients:

- Pizza dough
- 1/2 cup tomato sauce
- 1 1/2 cups shredded mozzarella cheese
- 1/2 cup sliced pepperoni
- Olive oil for drizzling

Instructions:

1. Preheat the oven to 475°F (245°C).
2. Roll out the pizza dough and spread a thin layer of tomato sauce.
3. Sprinkle shredded mozzarella cheese over the sauce.
4. Layer sliced pepperoni evenly over the cheese.
5. Bake for 10-12 minutes until the crust is golden and the cheese is melted and bubbling.
6. Drizzle with olive oil before serving.

Quattro Stagioni Pizza

Ingredients:

- Pizza dough
- 1/2 cup tomato sauce
- 1 1/2 cups shredded mozzarella
- 1/4 cup artichoke hearts, chopped
- 1/4 cup black olives, pitted and halved
- 1/4 cup cooked ham, chopped
- 1/4 cup mushrooms, sliced

Instructions:

1. Preheat the oven to 475°F (245°C).
2. Roll out the dough and spread tomato sauce evenly on top.
3. Sprinkle with mozzarella cheese, then divide the pizza into four sections.
4. Top each section with different ingredients: artichokes, olives, ham, and mushrooms.
5. Bake for 10-12 minutes, until the cheese is melted and the crust is golden.

Capricciosa Pizza

Ingredients:

- Pizza dough
- 1/2 cup tomato sauce
- 1 1/2 cups shredded mozzarella cheese
- 1/4 cup cooked ham, sliced
- 1/4 cup mushrooms, sliced
- 1/4 cup artichoke hearts, chopped
- 1/4 cup black olives, halved

Instructions:

1. Preheat the oven to 475°F (245°C).
2. Roll out the dough and spread a thin layer of tomato sauce.
3. Sprinkle mozzarella cheese over the sauce.
4. Add the toppings: ham, mushrooms, artichokes, and olives.
5. Bake for 10-12 minutes, or until the crust is golden and the cheese is bubbly.

Funghi Pizza

Ingredients:

- Pizza dough
- 1/2 cup tomato sauce
- 1 1/2 cups shredded mozzarella cheese
- 1 cup mushrooms, sliced
- Fresh parsley, chopped
- Olive oil for drizzling

Instructions:

1. Preheat the oven to 475°F (245°C).
2. Roll out the dough and spread a thin layer of tomato sauce.
3. Sprinkle with mozzarella cheese and add the sliced mushrooms.
4. Bake for 10-12 minutes, or until the cheese is melted and the mushrooms are tender.
5. Sprinkle with fresh parsley and drizzle with olive oil before serving.

Diavola Pizza

Ingredients:

- Pizza dough
- 1/2 cup tomato sauce
- 1 1/2 cups shredded mozzarella cheese
- 1/4 cup spicy salami or pepperoni, sliced
- Red chili flakes (optional)

Instructions:

1. Preheat the oven to 475°F (245°C).
2. Roll out the dough and spread a thin layer of tomato sauce.
3. Add the mozzarella cheese and layer the spicy salami or pepperoni on top.
4. Sprinkle red chili flakes for extra spice (optional).
5. Bake for 10-12 minutes until the crust is golden and the cheese is bubbly.

Napoletana Pizza

Ingredients:

- Pizza dough
- 1/2 cup tomato sauce
- 1 1/2 cups fresh mozzarella, sliced
- Anchovies, optional
- Fresh oregano leaves
- Olive oil for drizzling

Instructions:

1. Preheat the oven to 475°F (245°C).
2. Roll out the dough and spread tomato sauce over it.
3. Add the fresh mozzarella and place anchovies, if using, on top.
4. Sprinkle with fresh oregano leaves.
5. Bake for 10-12 minutes, or until the crust is golden and the cheese is bubbly.
6. Drizzle with olive oil before serving.

Prosciutto e Rucola Pizza

Ingredients:

- Pizza dough
- 1/2 cup tomato sauce
- 1 1/2 cups shredded mozzarella cheese
- 1/4 cup prosciutto, sliced
- Fresh arugula

Instructions:

1. Preheat the oven to 475°F (245°C).
2. Roll out the dough and spread a thin layer of tomato sauce.
3. Sprinkle with mozzarella cheese and bake for 10-12 minutes.
4. Once the pizza is out of the oven, top with prosciutto and fresh arugula.
5. Serve immediately.

Pizza Bianca with Ricotta and Spinach

Ingredients:

- Pizza dough
- 1/2 cup ricotta cheese
- 1 cup fresh spinach, sautéed
- 1/2 cup mozzarella cheese, shredded
- Olive oil for drizzling

Instructions:

1. Preheat the oven to 475°F (245°C).
2. Roll out the dough and spread a thin layer of ricotta cheese.
3. Top with sautéed spinach and mozzarella cheese.
4. Bake for 10-12 minutes, or until the crust is golden and the cheese is bubbly.
5. Drizzle with olive oil before serving.

Pizza Marinara

Ingredients:

- Pizza dough
- 1/2 cup tomato sauce
- 1 clove garlic, minced
- 1 teaspoon dried oregano
- Olive oil for drizzling

Instructions:

1. Preheat the oven to 475°F (245°C).
2. Roll out the dough and spread a thin layer of tomato sauce.
3. Sprinkle with minced garlic and oregano.
4. Bake for 10-12 minutes until the crust is golden.
5. Drizzle with olive oil before serving.

Pizza Siciliana

Ingredients:

- Pizza dough
- 1/2 cup tomato sauce
- 1 1/2 cups shredded mozzarella cheese
- 1/4 cup anchovies
- 1/4 cup capers
- 1/4 cup black olives, pitted and halved
- 1 small red onion, thinly sliced
- Fresh basil leaves

Instructions:

1. Preheat the oven to 475°F (245°C).
2. Roll out the dough and spread a thin layer of tomato sauce.
3. Add the shredded mozzarella cheese and top with anchovies, capers, olives, and red onion slices.
4. Bake for 10-12 minutes until the crust is golden and the cheese is bubbly.
5. Garnish with fresh basil leaves before serving.

Pizza Romana

Ingredients:

- Pizza dough
- 1/2 cup tomato sauce
- 1 1/2 cups shredded mozzarella cheese
- 1/4 cup cooked ham, sliced
- 1/4 cup black olives, pitted and halved
- Fresh rosemary

Instructions:

1. Preheat the oven to 475°F (245°C).
2. Roll out the dough and spread a thin layer of tomato sauce.
3. Top with mozzarella cheese, ham, and olives.
4. Sprinkle fresh rosemary over the pizza for extra flavor.
5. Bake for 10-12 minutes until the crust is golden and the cheese is melted and bubbly.

Pizza alla Puttanesca

Ingredients:

- Pizza dough
- 1/2 cup tomato sauce
- 1 1/2 cups shredded mozzarella cheese
- 1/4 cup anchovies
- 1/4 cup black olives, pitted and halved
- 1 tablespoon capers
- 2 cloves garlic, minced
- Red chili flakes (optional)

Instructions:

1. Preheat the oven to 475°F (245°C).
2. Roll out the dough and spread a thin layer of tomato sauce.
3. Sprinkle mozzarella cheese over the sauce.
4. Add anchovies, olives, capers, and minced garlic.
5. Bake for 10-12 minutes until the crust is golden and the cheese is bubbly.
6. Optionally, sprinkle with red chili flakes for some heat.

Veggie Supreme Pizza

Ingredients:

- Pizza dough
- 1/2 cup tomato sauce
- 1 1/2 cups shredded mozzarella cheese
- 1/4 cup red bell peppers, sliced
- 1/4 cup zucchini, sliced
- 1/4 cup mushrooms, sliced
- 1/4 cup black olives, pitted and halved
- Fresh spinach leaves

Instructions:

1. Preheat the oven to 475°F (245°C).
2. Roll out the dough and spread a thin layer of tomato sauce.
3. Top with mozzarella cheese and all the veggies (bell peppers, zucchini, mushrooms, olives).
4. Bake for 10-12 minutes until the cheese is melted and the veggies are tender.
5. Add fresh spinach leaves after baking.

Pizza al Salame

Ingredients:

- Pizza dough
- 1/2 cup tomato sauce
- 1 1/2 cups shredded mozzarella cheese
- 1/4 cup salami, sliced
- 1/4 cup red onion, thinly sliced
- Fresh oregano

Instructions:

1. Preheat the oven to 475°F (245°C).
2. Roll out the dough and spread a thin layer of tomato sauce.
3. Sprinkle mozzarella cheese on top and add salami slices and red onion.
4. Bake for 10-12 minutes until the cheese is golden and bubbly.
5. Garnish with fresh oregano leaves before serving.

Pizza al Pesto

Ingredients:

- Pizza dough
- 1/4 cup pesto sauce
- 1 1/2 cups shredded mozzarella cheese
- 1/4 cup sun-dried tomatoes, chopped
- 1/4 cup pine nuts
- Fresh arugula

Instructions:

1. Preheat the oven to 475°F (245°C).
2. Roll out the dough and spread pesto sauce evenly over the surface.
3. Sprinkle with mozzarella cheese and top with sun-dried tomatoes and pine nuts.
4. Bake for 10-12 minutes until the crust is golden and the cheese is bubbly.
5. Once out of the oven, top with fresh arugula.

Pizza Boscaiola

Ingredients:

- Pizza dough
- 1/2 cup tomato sauce
- 1 1/2 cups shredded mozzarella cheese
- 1/4 cup sausage, crumbled
- 1/4 cup mushrooms, sliced
- Fresh parsley

Instructions:

1. Preheat the oven to 475°F (245°C).
2. Roll out the dough and spread a thin layer of tomato sauce.
3. Add mozzarella cheese, sausage, and mushrooms.
4. Bake for 10-12 minutes until the crust is golden and the sausage is cooked through.
5. Garnish with fresh parsley before serving.

Pizza Rustica

Ingredients:

- Pizza dough
- 1/2 cup tomato sauce
- 1 1/2 cups shredded mozzarella cheese
- 1/4 cup cooked ham, sliced
- 1/4 cup artichoke hearts, chopped
- 1/4 cup black olives, pitted and halved
- Fresh rosemary

Instructions:

1. Preheat the oven to 475°F (245°C).
2. Roll out the dough and spread a thin layer of tomato sauce.
3. Top with mozzarella cheese, ham, artichokes, and olives.
4. Sprinkle with fresh rosemary.
5. Bake for 10-12 minutes until the crust is golden and the cheese is bubbly.

Calzone with Ricotta and Ham

Ingredients:

- Pizza dough
- 1/2 cup ricotta cheese
- 1/4 cup cooked ham, chopped
- 1/2 cup shredded mozzarella cheese
- 1 tablespoon grated Parmesan cheese
- 1 egg (for egg wash)

Instructions:

1. Preheat the oven to 475°F (245°C).
2. Roll out the dough into a round shape.
3. In the center, add ricotta, mozzarella, ham, and grated Parmesan.
4. Fold the dough over the filling to form a half-moon shape and seal the edges.
5. Brush the top with egg wash (1 beaten egg).
6. Bake for 15-20 minutes until golden and crispy.
7. Serve warm.

Pizza al Tartufo (Truffle Pizza)

Ingredients:

- Pizza dough
- 1/2 cup white sauce or crème fraîche
- 1 1/2 cups shredded mozzarella cheese
- 2 tablespoons truffle oil
- 1/4 cup fresh mushrooms, thinly sliced
- Fresh arugula for garnish
- Fresh Parmesan cheese, grated

Instructions:

1. Preheat the oven to 475°F (245°C).
2. Roll out the dough and spread a thin layer of white sauce or crème fraîche.
3. Sprinkle mozzarella cheese evenly over the sauce.
4. Arrange mushrooms on top and drizzle with truffle oil.
5. Bake for 10-12 minutes until the crust is golden and the cheese is melted.
6. Garnish with fresh arugula and a generous sprinkle of grated Parmesan.

Pizza Napoli with Anchovies

Ingredients:

- Pizza dough
- 1/2 cup tomato sauce
- 1 1/2 cups shredded mozzarella cheese
- 6-8 anchovy fillets, drained
- 1/4 cup black olives, pitted and halved
- Fresh oregano

Instructions:

1. Preheat the oven to 475°F (245°C).
2. Roll out the dough and spread a thin layer of tomato sauce.
3. Sprinkle mozzarella cheese over the sauce, and top with anchovies, olives, and fresh oregano.
4. Bake for 10-12 minutes until the cheese is bubbly and golden.
5. Serve hot, garnished with more oregano if desired.

Pizza con Gorgonzola e Pere (Gorgonzola and Pear Pizza)

Ingredients:

- Pizza dough
- 1/4 cup tomato sauce (optional, or use olive oil for a white pizza)
- 1 1/2 cups shredded mozzarella cheese
- 1/2 cup Gorgonzola cheese, crumbled
- 1 pear, thinly sliced
- 1 tablespoon honey
- Walnuts, chopped (optional)

Instructions:

1. Preheat the oven to 475°F (245°C).
2. Roll out the dough and spread a thin layer of tomato sauce or olive oil.
3. Top with mozzarella cheese, crumbled Gorgonzola, and pear slices.
4. Drizzle with honey and sprinkle walnuts on top (if using).
5. Bake for 10-12 minutes until the cheese is melted and golden.
6. Serve immediately, with a drizzle of extra honey if desired.

Pizza with Mushrooms and Truffle Oil

Ingredients:

- Pizza dough
- 1/2 cup tomato sauce or olive oil (for a white pizza)
- 1 1/2 cups shredded mozzarella cheese
- 1/2 cup mixed mushrooms, sliced
- 1 tablespoon truffle oil
- Fresh parsley, chopped

Instructions:

1. Preheat the oven to 475°F (245°C).
2. Roll out the dough and spread a thin layer of olive oil (or tomato sauce).
3. Sprinkle mozzarella cheese over the base.
4. Add the sliced mushrooms and drizzle with truffle oil.
5. Bake for 10-12 minutes until the crust is crispy and the cheese is melted.
6. Garnish with fresh chopped parsley before serving.

Pizza Margherita with Burrata

Ingredients:

- Pizza dough
- 1/2 cup tomato sauce
- 1 1/2 cups shredded mozzarella cheese
- 1 ball of burrata cheese
- Fresh basil leaves
- Olive oil for drizzling

Instructions:

1. Preheat the oven to 475°F (245°C).
2. Roll out the dough and spread a thin layer of tomato sauce.
3. Top with mozzarella cheese and bake for 10-12 minutes until the cheese is melted and golden.
4. Remove from the oven and place the burrata in the center.
5. Drizzle with olive oil and scatter fresh basil leaves on top.
6. Serve immediately with extra basil for garnish.

Pizza alla Caprese

Ingredients:

- Pizza dough
- 1/2 cup tomato sauce
- 1 1/2 cups shredded mozzarella cheese
- 2-3 ripe tomatoes, sliced
- Fresh basil leaves
- Olive oil for drizzling
- Balsamic glaze for drizzling (optional)

Instructions:

1. Preheat the oven to 475°F (245°C).
2. Roll out the dough and spread a thin layer of tomato sauce.
3. Top with mozzarella cheese and arrange the sliced tomatoes on top.
4. Bake for 10-12 minutes until the cheese is melted and the crust is golden.
5. Drizzle with olive oil, add fresh basil leaves, and optionally drizzle with balsamic glaze before serving.

Pizza with Sausage and Peppers

Ingredients:

- Pizza dough
- 1/2 cup tomato sauce
- 1 1/2 cups shredded mozzarella cheese
- 1/2 cup Italian sausage, cooked and crumbled
- 1/4 cup red bell peppers, sliced
- 1/4 cup yellow bell peppers, sliced
- Fresh parsley

Instructions:

1. Preheat the oven to 475°F (245°C).
2. Roll out the dough and spread a thin layer of tomato sauce.
3. Top with mozzarella cheese, cooked sausage, and bell pepper slices.
4. Bake for 10-12 minutes until the cheese is melted and bubbly.
5. Garnish with fresh parsley before serving.

Pizza alla Norma

Ingredients:

- Pizza dough
- 1/2 cup tomato sauce
- 1 1/2 cups shredded mozzarella cheese
- 1/2 eggplant, thinly sliced
- Fresh basil leaves
- Ricotta salata cheese, crumbled

Instructions:

1. Preheat the oven to 475°F (245°C).
2. Roll out the dough and spread a thin layer of tomato sauce.
3. Top with mozzarella cheese and layer with thin eggplant slices.
4. Bake for 10-12 minutes until the cheese is bubbly and the eggplant is tender.
5. Remove from the oven and sprinkle with ricotta salata and fresh basil before serving.

Pizza with Prosciutto di Parma and Figs

Ingredients:

- Pizza dough
- 1/2 cup tomato sauce or olive oil (for a white pizza)
- 1 1/2 cups shredded mozzarella cheese
- 4-5 fresh figs, quartered
- 4-5 slices Prosciutto di Parma
- Fresh arugula for garnish
- Balsamic reduction for drizzling

Instructions:

1. Preheat the oven to 475°F (245°C).
2. Roll out the dough and spread a thin layer of tomato sauce or olive oil.
3. Sprinkle with mozzarella cheese and arrange the quartered figs on top.
4. Bake for 10-12 minutes until the cheese is melted and golden.
5. After baking, top with Prosciutto di Parma, fresh arugula, and a drizzle of balsamic reduction.

Pizza with Grilled Vegetables

Ingredients:

- Pizza dough
- 1/2 cup tomato sauce
- 1 1/2 cups shredded mozzarella cheese
- 1/2 zucchini, sliced
- 1/2 red bell pepper, sliced
- 1/2 yellow bell pepper, sliced
- 1/4 red onion, thinly sliced
- Olive oil for drizzling
- Fresh basil leaves for garnish

Instructions:

1. Preheat the oven to 475°F (245°C).
2. Grill the zucchini, bell peppers, and onions on a grill pan until lightly charred.
3. Roll out the dough and spread a thin layer of tomato sauce.
4. Sprinkle with mozzarella cheese and arrange the grilled vegetables on top.
5. Drizzle with olive oil and bake for 10-12 minutes.
6. Garnish with fresh basil leaves before serving.

Pizza ai Quattro Formaggi (Four Cheese Pizza)

Ingredients:

- Pizza dough
- 1/2 cup tomato sauce (optional, for a white pizza use olive oil)
- 1/2 cup shredded mozzarella cheese
- 1/2 cup Gorgonzola cheese, crumbled
- 1/4 cup Parmesan cheese, grated
- 1/4 cup Fontina cheese, shredded
- Fresh rosemary for garnish

Instructions:

1. Preheat the oven to 475°F (245°C).
2. Roll out the dough and spread a thin layer of tomato sauce (if using).
3. Sprinkle the four cheeses evenly over the dough.
4. Bake for 10-12 minutes until the cheese is bubbly and golden.
5. Garnish with fresh rosemary before serving.

Pizza con Pomodorini e Basilico (Tomato and Basil Pizza)

Ingredients:

- Pizza dough
- 1/2 cup tomato sauce
- 1 1/2 cups shredded mozzarella cheese
- 10-12 cherry tomatoes, halved
- Fresh basil leaves
- Olive oil for drizzling

Instructions:

1. Preheat the oven to 475°F (245°C).
2. Roll out the dough and spread a thin layer of tomato sauce.
3. Sprinkle mozzarella cheese over the sauce, and arrange halved cherry tomatoes on top.
4. Bake for 10-12 minutes until the cheese is melted and the crust is golden.
5. Drizzle with olive oil and top with fresh basil leaves before serving.

Pizza with Smoked Salmon and Cream Cheese

Ingredients:

- Pizza dough
- 1/2 cup cream cheese, softened
- 1 1/2 cups shredded mozzarella cheese
- 4 oz smoked salmon, sliced
- 1 tablespoon capers
- Fresh dill for garnish
- Lemon wedges for serving

Instructions:

1. Preheat the oven to 475°F (245°C).
2. Roll out the dough and spread a thin layer of cream cheese.
3. Sprinkle with mozzarella cheese and bake for 10-12 minutes.
4. After baking, top with smoked salmon, capers, and fresh dill.
5. Serve with lemon wedges on the side.

Pizza with Eggplant and Mozzarella

Ingredients:

- Pizza dough
- 1/2 cup tomato sauce
- 1 1/2 cups shredded mozzarella cheese
- 1 eggplant, sliced
- Olive oil for drizzling
- Fresh basil leaves for garnish

Instructions:

1. Preheat the oven to 475°F (245°C).
2. Slice the eggplant and brush with olive oil. Grill or roast the slices until tender.
3. Roll out the dough and spread a thin layer of tomato sauce.
4. Sprinkle with mozzarella cheese and arrange the grilled eggplant on top.
5. Bake for 10-12 minutes and garnish with fresh basil leaves before serving.

Pizza with Pancetta and Pears

Ingredients:

- Pizza dough
- 1/2 cup tomato sauce or olive oil (for a white pizza)
- 1 1/2 cups shredded mozzarella cheese
- 6-8 slices pancetta
- 1 pear, thinly sliced
- Fresh arugula for garnish
- Honey for drizzling

Instructions:

1. Preheat the oven to 475°F (245°C).
2. Roll out the dough and spread a thin layer of tomato sauce or olive oil.
3. Top with mozzarella cheese, pancetta, and pear slices.
4. Bake for 10-12 minutes until the cheese is melted and the pancetta is crispy.
5. After baking, drizzle with honey and garnish with fresh arugula.

Pizza Capricciosa with Artichokes

Ingredients:

- Pizza dough
- 1/2 cup tomato sauce
- 1 1/2 cups shredded mozzarella cheese
- 6-8 slices cooked ham
- 1/4 cup marinated artichoke hearts, chopped
- 1/4 cup black olives, pitted and sliced
- Fresh oregano for garnish

Instructions:

1. Preheat the oven to 475°F (245°C).
2. Roll out the dough and spread a thin layer of tomato sauce.
3. Sprinkle with mozzarella cheese and top with ham, artichokes, and olives.
4. Bake for 10-12 minutes and garnish with fresh oregano before serving.

Pizza with Zucchini and Ricotta

Ingredients:

- Pizza dough
- 1/2 cup tomato sauce or olive oil (for a white pizza)
- 1 1/2 cups shredded mozzarella cheese
- 1 zucchini, thinly sliced
- 1/4 cup ricotta cheese
- Fresh basil for garnish

Instructions:

1. Preheat the oven to 475°F (245°C).
2. Roll out the dough and spread a thin layer of tomato sauce or olive oil.
3. Sprinkle with mozzarella cheese and arrange the zucchini slices on top.
4. Dot with small spoonfuls of ricotta cheese and bake for 10-12 minutes.
5. Garnish with fresh basil before serving.

Pizza with Sautéed Spinach and Garlic

Ingredients:

- Pizza dough
- 1/2 cup olive oil
- 1 1/2 cups shredded mozzarella cheese
- 2 cups fresh spinach, sautéed with garlic
- Fresh Parmesan cheese, grated
- Fresh nutmeg (optional)

Instructions:

1. Preheat the oven to 475°F (245°C).
2. Roll out the dough and spread a thin layer of olive oil.
3. Sprinkle with mozzarella cheese and top with sautéed spinach and garlic.
4. Bake for 10-12 minutes, then finish with a sprinkle of fresh Parmesan and grated nutmeg.

Pizza with Fennel and Sausage

Ingredients:

- Pizza dough
- 1/2 cup tomato sauce
- 1 1/2 cups shredded mozzarella cheese
- 1/2 fennel bulb, thinly sliced
- 1/2 cup Italian sausage, cooked and crumbled
- Fresh rosemary for garnish

Instructions:

1. Preheat the oven to 475°F (245°C).
2. Roll out the dough and spread a thin layer of tomato sauce.
3. Sprinkle with mozzarella cheese and top with fennel slices and cooked sausage.
4. Bake for 10-12 minutes and garnish with fresh rosemary before serving.

Pizza alla Salsiccia e Friarielli (Sausage and Broccoli Rabe Pizza)

Ingredients:

- Pizza dough
- 1/2 cup tomato sauce
- 1 1/2 cups shredded mozzarella cheese
- 1 Italian sausage link, removed from casing and crumbled
- 1 cup broccoli rabe (friarielli), sautéed
- Fresh chili flakes (optional)
- Olive oil for drizzling

Instructions:

1. Preheat the oven to 475°F (245°C).
2. Roll out the dough and spread a thin layer of tomato sauce.
3. Sprinkle with mozzarella cheese.
4. Cook the sausage in a pan until browned and crumbly. Sauté the broccoli rabe until tender.
5. Top the pizza with cooked sausage and sautéed broccoli rabe.
6. Bake for 10-12 minutes until golden, then drizzle with olive oil and chili flakes (optional) before serving.

Pizza con Radicchio e Gorgonzola (Radicchio and Gorgonzola Pizza)

Ingredients:

- Pizza dough
- 1/2 cup olive oil
- 1 1/2 cups shredded mozzarella cheese
- 1/2 cup Gorgonzola cheese, crumbled
- 1/2 small radicchio, thinly sliced
- 1/4 cup walnuts, chopped
- Honey for drizzling (optional)

Instructions:

1. Preheat the oven to 475°F (245°C).
2. Roll out the dough and brush with olive oil.
3. Sprinkle mozzarella cheese evenly over the dough.
4. Arrange radicchio slices on top and crumble Gorgonzola cheese over the pizza.
5. Scatter walnuts over the top and bake for 10-12 minutes.
6. Once out of the oven, drizzle with a bit of honey for a sweet finish.

Pizza with Fresh Basil and Mozzarella

Ingredients:

- Pizza dough
- 1/2 cup tomato sauce
- 1 1/2 cups fresh mozzarella, sliced
- Fresh basil leaves
- Olive oil for drizzling
- Balsamic glaze (optional)

Instructions:

1. Preheat the oven to 475°F (245°C).
2. Roll out the dough and spread a thin layer of tomato sauce.
3. Arrange the fresh mozzarella slices evenly on the pizza.
4. Bake for 10-12 minutes until the cheese is bubbly and the crust is golden.
5. Once baked, add fresh basil leaves and drizzle with olive oil or balsamic glaze.

Pizza ai Frutti di Mare (Seafood Pizza)

Ingredients:

- Pizza dough
- 1/2 cup tomato sauce or olive oil (for a white pizza)
- 1 1/2 cups shredded mozzarella cheese
- 1/4 cup shrimp, peeled and deveined
- 1/4 cup squid rings
- 1/4 cup mussels, cleaned
- 2 cloves garlic, minced
- Fresh parsley for garnish
- Lemon wedges for serving

Instructions:

1. Preheat the oven to 475°F (245°C).
2. Roll out the dough and spread a thin layer of tomato sauce or olive oil.
3. Sprinkle with mozzarella cheese.
4. Cook the seafood briefly in a hot pan with garlic until just cooked.
5. Top the pizza with the seafood and bake for 10-12 minutes.
6. Garnish with fresh parsley and serve with lemon wedges.

Pizza with Sweet Potatoes and Goat Cheese

Ingredients:

- Pizza dough
- 1/2 cup olive oil
- 1 1/2 cups shredded mozzarella cheese
- 1 small sweet potato, thinly sliced
- 1/4 cup goat cheese, crumbled
- Fresh thyme for garnish
- Salt and pepper to taste

Instructions:

1. Preheat the oven to 475°F (245°C).
2. Roll out the dough and brush with olive oil.
3. Arrange the thinly sliced sweet potatoes evenly on the dough.
4. Sprinkle with mozzarella cheese and crumbled goat cheese.
5. Bake for 10-12 minutes until the cheese is melted and the sweet potatoes are tender.
6. Garnish with fresh thyme and season with salt and pepper.

Pizza with Roasted Red Peppers and Olives

Ingredients:

- Pizza dough
- 1/2 cup tomato sauce
- 1 1/2 cups shredded mozzarella cheese
- 1/2 cup roasted red peppers, sliced
- 1/4 cup black olives, pitted and sliced
- Fresh oregano for garnish
- Olive oil for drizzling

Instructions:

1. Preheat the oven to 475°F (245°C).
2. Roll out the dough and spread a thin layer of tomato sauce.
3. Sprinkle mozzarella cheese over the dough and top with roasted red peppers and olives.
4. Bake for 10-12 minutes until golden.
5. Drizzle with olive oil and garnish with fresh oregano before serving.

Pizza with Chicken and Pesto

Ingredients:

- Pizza dough
- 1/2 cup pesto sauce (store-bought or homemade)
- 1 1/2 cups shredded mozzarella cheese
- 1 cooked chicken breast, thinly sliced
- Cherry tomatoes, halved
- Fresh basil leaves for garnish
- Olive oil for drizzling

Instructions:

1. Preheat the oven to 475°F (245°C).
2. Roll out the pizza dough and spread a layer of pesto sauce over the surface.
3. Top with shredded mozzarella cheese and arrange the sliced chicken and cherry tomatoes on top.
4. Bake for 10-12 minutes until the cheese is bubbly and golden.
5. Once out of the oven, garnish with fresh basil leaves and drizzle with a little olive oil.

Pizza Margherita with Arugula

Ingredients:

- Pizza dough
- 1/2 cup tomato sauce
- 1 1/2 cups fresh mozzarella cheese, sliced
- Fresh arugula leaves
- Olive oil for drizzling
- Balsamic glaze (optional)

Instructions:

1. Preheat the oven to 475°F (245°C).
2. Roll out the dough and spread a thin layer of tomato sauce.
3. Place the fresh mozzarella slices evenly on top of the sauce.
4. Bake for 10-12 minutes until the cheese is melted and the crust is golden.
5. Once baked, top with fresh arugula leaves and drizzle with olive oil and balsamic glaze (if using).

Pizza with Speck and Apples

Ingredients:

- Pizza dough
- 1/2 cup crème fraîche or ricotta
- 1 1/2 cups shredded mozzarella cheese
- 1/4 cup speck (smoked prosciutto), sliced
- 1 small apple, thinly sliced (preferably a tart variety like Granny Smith)
- Fresh rosemary for garnish
- Olive oil for drizzling

Instructions:

1. Preheat the oven to 475°F (245°C).
2. Roll out the dough and spread a layer of crème fraîche or ricotta over it.
3. Sprinkle with shredded mozzarella cheese, then arrange the thin apple slices and speck over the top.
4. Bake for 10-12 minutes until the cheese is golden and bubbly.
5. Once out of the oven, garnish with fresh rosemary and drizzle with a little olive oil.

Pizza alla Diavola with Chili Peppers

Ingredients:

- Pizza dough
- 1/2 cup tomato sauce
- 1 1/2 cups shredded mozzarella cheese
- 1/4 cup spicy salami (like pepperoni or 'nduja), sliced
- 1-2 fresh chili peppers, sliced
- Fresh basil leaves for garnish
- Olive oil for drizzling

Instructions:

1. Preheat the oven to 475°F (245°C).
2. Roll out the dough and spread a thin layer of tomato sauce.
3. Sprinkle with shredded mozzarella cheese, then top with spicy salami and chili pepper slices.
4. Bake for 10-12 minutes until the cheese is melted and the crust is crispy.
5. Once out of the oven, garnish with fresh basil leaves and drizzle with olive oil.

Pizza with Ricotta, Honey, and Pistachios

Ingredients:

- Pizza dough
- 1/2 cup ricotta cheese
- 1 1/2 cups shredded mozzarella cheese
- 1/4 cup pistachios, chopped
- 2-3 tablespoons honey
- Fresh thyme or rosemary for garnish

Instructions:

1. Preheat the oven to 475°F (245°C).
2. Roll out the dough and spread a layer of ricotta cheese.
3. Sprinkle with shredded mozzarella cheese and chopped pistachios.
4. Bake for 10-12 minutes until the cheese is golden and the crust is crispy.
5. Once out of the oven, drizzle with honey and garnish with fresh thyme or rosemary.

Pizza with Roasted Garlic and Parmesan

Ingredients:

- Pizza dough
- 1/2 cup olive oil
- 1 bulb garlic, roasted and mashed
- 1 1/2 cups shredded mozzarella cheese
- 1/4 cup grated Parmesan cheese
- Fresh parsley for garnish
- Salt and pepper to taste

Instructions:

1. Preheat the oven to 475°F (245°C).
2. Roll out the dough and brush with olive oil.
3. Spread the roasted garlic over the dough, then sprinkle with mozzarella and Parmesan cheese.
4. Bake for 10-12 minutes until the cheese is melted and golden.
5. Once baked, season with salt and pepper, garnish with fresh parsley, and serve.